BALDESAR CASTIGLIONE

ETIQUETTE FOR RENAISSANCE GENTLEMEN

TRANSLATED BY GEORGE BULL

PENGUIN BOOKS

PENGUIN BOOKS

Published by the Penguin Group
Penguin Books Ltd, 27 Wrights Lane, London w8 5TZ, England
Penguin Books USA Inc., 375 Hudson Street, New York, New York 10014, USA
Penguin Books Australia Ltd, Ringwood, Victoria, Australia
Penguin Books Canada Ltd, 10 Alcorn Avenue, Toronto, Ontario, Canada M4V 3B2
Penguin Books (NZ) Ltd, 182–190 Wairau Road, Auckland 10, New Zealand

Penguin Books Ltd, Registered Offices: Harmondsworth, Middlesex, England

This selection is from George Bull's translation of
The Book of the Courtier, published in Penguin Classics 1967
This edition published 1995
1 3 5 7 9 10 8 6 4 2

Printed in England by Clays Ltd, St Ives plc

I have spent a long time wondering, my dear Alfonso, which of two things was the more difficult for me: either to refuse what you have asked me so often and so insistently, or to do it. On the one hand, it seemed to me to be very hard to refuse anything, and especially something praiseworthy, to one whom I love dearly and by whom I feel I am very dearly loved; yet on the other hand, to embark on a project which I was uncertain of being able to finish seemed wrong to one who respects adverse criticism as much as it ought to be respected. Eventually, after a great deal of thought, I have made up my mind to find out how diligent I can be when helped by affection and the anxiety to please, which usually act as a sharp spur to all kinds of activity.

Now your request is that I should describe what, in my view, is the form of courtiership most appropriate for a gentleman living at the Courts of princes, by which he will have the knowledge and the ability to serve them in every reasonable thing, winning their favour and the praise of others. In short, you want to know what kind of man must be one who deserves the name of a perfect courtier and has no shortcomings whatsoever. Considering this request, I must say that, if I did not think it a greater fault to be judged wanting in love by you than wanting in prudence by others, I would have rejected the task, for fear of being accused of rashness by all those who know how difficult an undertaking it is to select from all the many and various customs followed at the Courts of Christendom the most perfect model and, as it were, the very flower of courtiership. For familiarity often causes the same things to be liked and disliked: and thus it sometimes happens that the customs, behaviour, ceremonies and ways of life approved of at one period of time grow to be looked down on, and those which were once looked down on come to be approved. So we can see clearly enough that usage is more effective than reason in introducing new things among us and in wiping out the old. And anyone who tries to judge what is perfect in these matters often deceives himself. Being well aware of this, therefore, and of the many other problems connected with the subject proposed to me, I am compelled to say something by way of excuse and to testify that what I am doing wrong (if it can be called so) you are responsible for as well, and that if I am to be blamed for it you must share the blame. After all, you must be judged to be as much at fault in imposing on me a task greater than my resources as I am in having accepted it.

But let us now begin to discuss the subject we have chosen and, if it is possible, create a courtier so perfect that the prince who is worthy of his service, even though his dominion is small, can count himself a truly great ruler. In these books we shall not follow any strict order or list a series of precepts, as is the normal practice in teaching. Instead, following many writers of the ancient world, and reviving a pleasant memory, we shall recount some discussions which once took place among men who were singularly qualified in these matters. Even though I did not take part in them in person (being in England when they were held), they were faithfully reported to me soon after my return by someone who was present, and I shall endeavour to reproduce them as accurately as my memory allows so that you may discover what was held and thought on the subject by eminent men whose judgement can always be trusted completely. Nor will it be beside the purpose, in order to continue the story in logical order, to describe the occasion of the discussions that took place.

On the slopes of the Apennines, almost in the centre of Italy towards the Adriatic, is situated, as everyone knows, the little city of Urbino. Although it is surrounded by hills which are perhaps not as agreeable as those found in many other places, none the less it has been favoured by Nature with a very rich and fertile countryside, so that as well as a salubrious atmosphere it enjoys an abundance of all the necessities of life. Among the blessings and advantages that can be claimed for it, I believe the greatest is that for a long time now it has been governed by outstanding rulers, even though in the turmoils into which Italy was plunged by war it was for a time deprived of them. Without looking further, we can find a splendid example in Duke Federico of glorious memory, who in his day was the light of Italy. Nor are there lacking today any number of reliable witnesses to his prudence, humanity, justice, generosity and unconquerable spirit, and to his military skill, which was brilliantly attested by his many victories, his ability to capture impregnable places, his swift and decisive expeditions, his having routed many times with few troops great and formidable armies, and his never having lost a single battle. So we can fairly compare him with many famous men of the ancient world. Among his other commendable enterprises, Duke Federico built on the rugged site of Urbino a palace which many believe to be the most beautiful in all Italy; and he furnished it so well and appropriately that it seemed more like a city than a mere palace. For he adorned it not only with the usual objects, such as silver vases, wall-hangings of the richest cloth of gold, silk and other similar material, but also with countless antique statues of marble and bronze, with rare pictures, and with every kind of musical instrument; nor would he tolerate anything that was not most rare and outstanding. Then, at great cost, he collected a large number of the finest and rarest books, in Greek, Latin and Hebrew, all of which he adorned with gold and silver, believing that they were the crowning glory of his great palace.

Following, therefore, the course of Nature, and being already sixty-five years old, Duke Federico died as gloriously as he had lived, leaving as his heir his only son, a little, motherless boy of ten named Guidobaldo. And Guidobaldo seemed to inherit not only his father's state but all his virtues as well, immediately showing in his marvellous disposition the promise of more than can be expected from a mortal man. In consequence, it was widely said that of all the wonderful things that Duke Federico had done, the greatest was to have fathered such a son. But envious of his great qualities, Fortune set herself with all her might to frustrate what had begun so nobly, with the result that before he was yet twenty years old Duke Guido fell sick with the gout which, inflicting terrible pain, grew steadily worse and within a short space of time crippled him so badly that he could neither stand nor walk. Thus one of the best and most handsome men in the whole world was deformed and ruined while still of tender age. Not satisfied even with this, Fortune so opposed him in all his projects that he rarely succeeded in what he undertook; and although he was a man of mature deliberation and unconquerable spirit, everything he set his hand to, whether in arms or anything else, great or small, always ended unhappily, as we can see from the many diverse calamities which befell him, and which he always bore with such fortitude that his will was never crushed by fate. On the contrary, with great resilience and spirit, he despised the blows of Fortune, living the life of a healthy and happy man, despite sickness and adversity, and achieving true dignity and universal renown. Thus even though he was infirm, he campaigned with a most honourable rank in the service of their Serene Highnesses Kings Alfonso and Ferdinand the Younger of Naples, and subsequently with Pope Alexander VI as well as the Signories of Venice and Florence. Then, after the accession of Pope Julius II, he was made Captain of the Church; and during this time, following his customary style of life, he saw to it that his household was filled with very noble and worthy gentlemen, with whom he lived on the most familiar terms, delighting in their company. In this the pleasure he caused

5

others was no less than what he received, for he was very well versed in both Latin and Greek, and possessed as well as an affable and charming nature, an infinite range of knowledge. Moreover, his indomitable spirit so spurred him on that, even though he himself was unable to take part in chivalrous activities, as he once used to, he loved to see them pursued by others, and he would show his fine judgement when commenting on what they did, correcting or praising each one according to his merits. So in jousts and tournaments, in riding, in handling every kind of weapon, as well as in the festivities, games and musical performances, in short, in all the activities appropriate to a well-born gentleman, everyone at his Court strove to behave in such a way as to deserve to be judged worthy of the Duke's noble company.

So all day and every day at the Court of Urbino was spent on honourable and pleasing activities both of the body and the mind. But since the Duke always retired to his bedroom soon after supper, because of his infirmity, as a rule at that hour everyone went to join the Duchess, Elisabetta Gonzaga, with whom was always to be found signora Emilia Pia, a lady gifted with such a lively wit and judgement, as you know, that she seemed to be in command of all and to endow everyone else with her own discernment and goodness. In their company polite conversations and innocent pleasantries were heard, and everyone's face was so full of laughter and gaiety that the house could truly be called the very in of happiness. And I am sure that the delight and enjoyment to be had from loving and devoted companionship were never experi-

6

enced elsewhere as they once were in Urbino. For, apart from the honour it was for each of us to be in the service of a ruler such as I described above, we all felt supremely happy whenever we came into the presence of the Duchess; and this sense of contentment formed between us a bond of affection so strong that even between brothers there could never have been such harmonious agreement and heartfelt love as there was among us all. It was the same with the ladies, whose company we all enjoyed very freely and innocently, since everyone was allowed to talk and sit, make jokes and laugh with whom he pleased, though such was the respect we had for the wishes of the Duchess that the liberty we enjoyed was accompanied by the most careful restraint. And without exception everyone considered that the most pleasurable thing possible was to please her and the most displeasing thing in the world was to earn her displeasure. So for these reasons in her company the most decorous behaviour proved compatible with the greatest freedom, and in her presence our games and laughter were seasoned both with the sharpest witticisms and with a gracious and sober dignity. For the modesty and nobility which informed every act, word and gesture of the Duchess, in jest and laughter, caused even those seeing her for the first time to recognize that she was a very great lady. It seemed, from the way in which she influenced those around her, that she tempered us all to her own character and quality, so that everyone endeavoured to imitate her personal way of behaviour, deriving as it were a model of fine manners from the presence of so great and talented a woman, whose high qualities I do not intend to describe now, since this is not to my purpose and they are well known to all the world, apart from being beyond the reach of whatever I could say or write. But I must add that those qualities in the Duchess which might have remained somewhat hidden, Fortune, as if admiring such rare virtues, chose to reveal through many adversities and harsh blows, in order to demonstrate that in the tender soul of a woman, and accompanied by singular beauty, there may also dwell prudence and a courageous spirit and all those virtues very rarely found even in the staunchest of men.

To continue, let me say that it was the custom for all the gentlemen of the house to go, immediately after supper, to the rooms of the Duchess; and there, along with pleasant recreations and enjoyments of various kinds, including constant music and dancing, sometimes intriguing questions were asked, and sometimes ingenious games played (now on the suggestion of one person and now of another) in which, using various ways of concealment, those present revealed their thoughts in allegories to this person or that. And occasionally, there would be discussions on various subjects, or there would be a sharp exchange of spontaneous witticisms; and often 'emblems', as we call them nowadays, were devised for the occasion. And everyone enjoyed these exchanges immensely, since, as I have said, the house was full of very noble and talented persons, among whom, as you know, the most famous was signor Ottaviano Fregoso, his brother Federico, the Magnifico Giuliano de' Medici, Pietro Bembo, Cesare Gonzaga, Count Lodovico da Canossa, Gaspare Pallavicino, signor Lodovico Pio, signor Morello da Ortona, Pietro da Napoli, Roberto da Bari and countless other high-born gentlemen. There were also many who, although they did not as a rule stay permanently, yet spent most of their time there: they included Bernardo Bibbiena, the Unico Aretino, Giovan Cristoforo Romano, Pietro Monte, Terpandro and Nicolò Frisio. So gathered together at the Court of Urbino there were always to be found poets, musicians, buffoons of all kinds, and the finest talent of every description anywhere in Italy. . . .

Looks and Appearance

After the Count had fallen silent for a moment, Bernardo Bibbiena said, with a smile:

'I remember your saying earlier that this courtier of ours should be naturally endowed with beauty of countenance and person and with an attractive grace. Well, I feel sure that I possess both grace and beauty of countenance, and that's why so many women, as you know, are madly in love with me. But when it comes to the beauty of my person, I am rather doubtful, and especially as regards these legs of mine which do not seem to me to be as good as I would wish; still, as to my chest and so on, I am quite satisfied. So please explain in more detail about what shape of body one should have, so that I can extricate myself from doubt and put my mind at rest.'

After everyone had laughed at this for a moment, the Count said:

'Certainly it's no lie to say that you possess the grace of countenance that I mentioned, and I have no need of any other example to illustrate it; for undoubtedly we can see that your appearance is very agreeable and pleasing to all, even if your features are not very delicate, though then again you mange to appear both manly and graceful. This is a quality found in many different kinds of faces. And I would like our courtier to have the same aspect. I don't want him to appear soft and feminine as so many try to do, when they not only curl their hair and pluck their eyebrows but also preen themselves like the most wanton and dissolute creatures imaginable. Indeed, they appear so effeminate and languid in the way they walk, or stand, or do anything at all, that their limbs look as if they are about to fall apart; and they pronounce their words in such a drawling way that it seems as if they are about to expire on the spot. And the more they find themselves in the company of men of rank, the more they carry on like that. Since Nature has not in fact made them the ladies they want to seem and be, they should be treated not as honest women but as common whores and be driven out from all gentlemanly society, let alone the Courts of great lords.

'Then, as for the physical appearance of the courtier, I would say that all that is necessary is that he should be neither too small nor too big, since either of these two conditions causes a certain contemptuous wonder and men built in this way are stared at as if they were monsters. However, if one is forced to chose between the two evils, then it is better to be on the small side than unduly large; for men who are so huge are often found to be rather thickheaded, and moreover, they are also unsuited for sport and recreation, which I think most important for the courtier. So I wish our courtier to be well built, with finely proportioned members, and I would have him demonstrate strength and lightness and suppleness and be good at all the physical exercises befitting a warrior. Here, I believe, his first duty is to know how to handle expertly every kind of weapon, either on foot or mounted, to understand all their finer points, and to be especially well informed about all those weapons commonly used among gentlemen. For apart from their use in war, when perhaps the finer points may be neglected, often differences arise between one gentleman and another and lead to duels, and very often the weapons used are those that come immediately to hand. So, for safety's sake, it is important to know about them. And I am not one of those who assert that all skill is forgotten in a fight; because anyone who loses his skill at such a time shows that he has allowed his fear to rob him of his courage and his wits.

SPORTS AND GAMES

'I also believe that it is of the highest importance to know how to wrestle, since this often accompanies combat on foot. Next, both for his own sake and for his friends, the courtier should understand about seeking restitution and the conduct of disputes, and he should be skilled in seizing the advantage, and in all this he must show both courage and prudence. Nor should he be too anxious for these engagements, save when his honour demands it; for, as well as the considerable danger that an uncertain outcome brings with it, whoever rushes into these things precipitately and without urgent cause deserves to be gravely censured, even if he is successful. However, when a man has committed himself so far that he cannot withdraw without reproach then both in the preliminaries and in the duel itself he should be very deliberate. He should always show readiness and courage; and he should not behave like those who are always quibbling and arguing over points of honour, and when they have the choice of weapons, select those which can neither cut nor prick, arm themselves as if they had to face a cannonade, and, thinking it enough if they are not defeated, retreat all the time and keep in the defensive, giving proof of utter cowardice, and in this way making themselves the sport of children, like those two men from Ancona who fought at Perugia a little while ago, and made everyone who saw them burst out laughing.'

'And who were they?' asked Gaspare Pallavicino.

'Two cousins,' answered Cesare.

'And in their fighting, more like two dear brothers,' said the Count. Then he continued:

'Weapons are also often used in various sports during peacetime, and gentlemen often perform in public spectacles before the people and before ladies and great lords. So I wish our courtier to be an accomplished and versatile horseman and, as well as having a knowledge of horses and all the matters to do with riding, he should put every effort and diligence into surpassing the rest just a little in everything, so that he may always be recognized as superior. And as we read of Alcibiades, that he surpassed all those peoples among whom he lived, and each time in regard to what they claimed to be best at, so this courtier of ours should outstrip all others, and in regard to the things they know well. Thus it is the peculiar excellence of the Italians to ride well with the rein, to handle spirited horses very skilfully, and to tilt and joust; so in all this the courtier should compare with the best of them. In tourneys, in holding his ground, in forcing his way forward, he should compare with the best of the French; in volleying, in running bulls, in casting spears and darts, he should be outstanding among the Spaniards. But, above all, he should accompany his every act with a certain grace and fine judgement if he wishes to earn that universal regard which everyone covets.

'There are also many other sports which, although they do not directly require the use of weapons, are closely related to arms and demand a great deal of manly exertion. Among these it seems to me that hunting is the most important, since in many ways it resembles warfare; moreover, it is the true pastime of great lords, it is a suitable pursuit for a courtier, and we know that it was very popular in the ancient world. It is also fitting that the courtier should know how to swim, jump, run and cast the stone for, apart from the usefulness of these accomplishments in war, one if often required to display one's skill and such sports can help to build up a good reputation, especially with the crowd which the courtier always has to humour. Another noble sport which is very suitable for the courtier to play is tennis, for this shows how well he is built physically, how quick and agile he is in every member, and whether he has all the qualities demonstrated in most other games. I think no less highly of performing on horseback, which is certainly very exhausting and difficult but more than anything else serves to make a man wonderfully agile and dextrous; and apart from its usefulness, if agility on horseback is accompanied by gracefulness, in my opinion it makes a finer spectacle than any other sport. Then if our courtier possesses more than average skill in all these sports, I think he should ignore the others, such as turning cartwheels, tight-rope walking and that kind of thing, since these are more like acrobatics and hardly suitable for a gentleman. Then again, since one cannot always be taking part in such strenuous exercises (besides which constant repetition causes satiety and destroys the regard we have for rare things) one must always be sure to give variety to the way one lives by doing different things. So I would like the courtier sometimes to descend to calmer and more restful games, and to escape envy and enter pleasantly into the company of all the others by doing everything they do; although he should never fail to behave in a commendable manner and should rule all his actions with that good judgement which will not allow him to take part in any foolishness. Let him laugh, jest, banter, romp and dance, though in a fashion that always reflects good sense and discretion, and let him say and do everything with grace.' . . .

THE ART OF PAINTING

'Before we launch into this subject,' the Count replied, 'I should like us to discuss something else again which, since I consider it highly important, I think our courtier should certainly not neglect: and this is the question of drawing and of the art of painting itself. And do not be surprised that I demand this ability, even if nowadays it may appear mechanical and hardly suited to a gentleman. For I recall having read that in the ancient world, and in Greece especially, children of gentle birth were required to learn painting at school, as a worthy and necessary accomplishment, and it was ranked among the foremost of the liberal arts; subsequently, a public law was passed forbidding it to be taught to slaves. It was also held in great honour among the Romans, and from it the very noble family of the Fabii took its name, for the first Fabius was called *Pictor*. He was, indeed, an outstanding painter, and so devoted to the art that when he painted the walls of the Temple of Salus he signed his name: this was because (despite his having been born into an illustrious family, honoured by so many consular titles, triumphs and other dignities, and despite the fact that he himself was a man of letters, learned in law and numbered among the orators) Fabius believed that he could enhance his name and reputation by leaving a memorial pointing out that he had also been a painter. And there was no lack of celebrated painters belonging to other illustrious families. In fact, from painting, which is in itself a most worthy and noble art, many useful skills can be derived, and not least for military purposes: thus a knowledge of the art gives one the facility to sketch towns, rivers, bridges, citadels, fortresses and similar things, which otherwise cannot be shown to others even if, with a great deal of effort, the details are memorized. To be sure, anyone who does not esteem the art of painting seems to me to be quite wrong-headed. For when all is said and done, the very fabric of the universe, which we can contemplate in the vast spaces of heaven, so resplendent with their shining stars, in the earth at its centre, girdled by the seas, varied with mountains, rivers and valleys, and adorned with so many different varieties of trees, lovely flowers and grasses, can be said to be a great and noble painting, composed by Nature and the hand of God. And, in my opinion, whoever can imitate it deserves the highest praise. Nor is such imitation achieved without the knowledge of many things, as anyone who attempts the task well knows. Therefore in the ancient world both painting and painters were held in the greatest respect, and the art itself was brought to the highest pitch of excellence. Of this, a sure proof is to be found in the ancient marble and bronze statues which still survive; for although painting differs from sculpture, both the one and the other derive from the same source, namely from good designs. So if the statues which have come down to us are inspired works of art we may readily believe that so, too, were the paintings of the ancient world; indeed, they must have been still more so, because they required greater artistry.'

Then signora Emilia, turning to Giovan Cristoforo Romano, who was seated with the others, asked him:

'What do you think of this opinion? Would you agree that painting allows for greater artistry than sculpture?'

'Madam,' replied Giovan Cristoforo, 'I maintain that sculpture requires more effort and more skill than painting, and possesses greater dignity.'

The Count then remarked:

'Certainly statues are more durable, so perhaps they may be said to prove more dignified; for since they are intended for monuments, they serve the purpose for which they are made better than paintings. But, leaving aside the question of commemoration, both painting and sculpture also serve a decorative purpose, and in this regard painting is far superior. And if it is not, so to say, as enduring as sculpture, all the same it survives a long time, and for as long as it does so it is far more beautiful.'

Then Giovan Cristoforo replied:

'I truly believe that you are not saying what you really think, and this solely for the sake of your Raphael; and perhaps, as well, you feel that the excellence you perceive in his work as a painter is so supreme that it cannot be rivalled by any sculpture in marble. But remember that this is praise for the artist and not for his art.'

Then he continued:

'Indeed, I willingly accept that both painting and sculpture are skilful imitations of Nature; yet I still do not understand how you can maintain that what is real and is Nature's own creation cannot be more faithfully copied in a bronze or marble figure, in which all members are rounded, fashioned and proportioned just as Nature makes them, than in a picture, consisting of a flat surface

17

and colours that deceive the eye. And don't tell me that being is not nearer the truth than merely seeming to be. Moreover, I maintain that working in stone is far more difficult, because if a mistake is made it cannot be remedied, seeing that repairs are impossible with marble, and the figure must be started again; whereas this is not the case with painting, which can be gone over a thousand times, being improved all the time as parts of the picture are added to or removed.'

The Painter's Skill

Then, with a smile, the Count replied:

'I am not arguing for the sake of Raphael, nor should you think me so ignorant as not to recognize the excellence shown by Michelangelo and yourself and other sculptors. But I am speaking of the art and not the artists. You say truly enough that both painting and sculpture are imitations of Nature; but it is not the case that the one seems to be what it portrays and the other really is so. For although statues are made in the round, like objects in real life, and painting is seen only on the surface, sculpture lacks many things to be found in painting, and especially light and shade: for example, the natural colouring of the flesh, which appears altogether changed in marble, the painter copies faithfully, using more or less light and shade according to need, which the sculptor cannot do. And even though the painter does not fashion his figures in the round, he does depict the muscles and members of the body rounded and merging into the unseen parts of his fingers in such a way as to demonstrate his knowledge and understanding of these as well. The painter requires still greater skill in depicting members that are foreshortened and taper gradually away from the point of vision, on the principles of perspective. This, by means of proportioned lines, colours, light and shade, simulates foreground and distance on an upright surface, to the degree that the painter wishes. Does it, then, seem of little importance to you that Nature's colours can be reproduced in flesh-tints, in clothing and in all the other objects that are coloured in life? This is something the sculptor cannot do. Still less can he depict the love-light in a person's eyes, with their black or blue colouring; the colour of blond hair; the gleam of weapons; the darkness of night; a tempest at sea; thunder and lightning; a city in conflagration; or the break of rosy dawn with its rays of gold and red. In short, it is beyond his powers to depict sky, sea, land, mountains, woods, meadows, gardens, rivers, cities or houses; but not beyond the powers of the painter.

'So it seems to me that painting is nobler and allows of greater artistry than sculpture, and I believe that in the ancient world it reached the same perfection as other things; and this we can see from a few surviving works, especially in the catacombs in Rome, but far more clearly from the evidence of classical literature, which contains so many admiring references to both painting and painters, and informs us of the high esteem in which they were held by governments and rulers. For example, we read that Alexander was so fond of Apelles of Ephesus that once, after he had had him portray one of his favourite mistresses, and then heard that the worthy painter had fallen desperately in love with her marvellous beauty, without a second thought he gave the woman to him: this was an act of generosity truly worthy of Alexander, to give away not only treasures and states but his own affections and desires; and it showed, too, how deeply fond he was of Apelles, to please whom he cared nothing about the displeasure of the lady whom he loved so much himself, and who, we may well believe, was more than grieved to lose so great a king in exchange for a painter. Many instances are recorded of Alexander's kindness towards Apelles; but the clearest evidence of his esteem for him is seen in the decree he issued that no other painter should dare to do his portrait. Here I could tell you of the contests of so many noble painters, who were the admiration and wonder of the world; I could tell you of the magnificence with which the ancient emperors adorned their triumphs with pictures, dedicated them in public places, and acquired them as cherished possessions; I could tell you how some painters have been know to give their pictures away, believing that they could not be adequately paid for with gold or silver; and how a painting by Protogenes was so highly regarded that when Demetrius was laying siege to Rhodes and could have entered the city by setting fire to the quarter where he knew the painting was, rather than cause it to be burned he called off the attack, and so failed to take the place; and how Metrodorus, an outstanding painter and philosopher, was sent by the Athenians to Lucius Paulus to teach his children and to decorate the triumph that he had to make. Moreover, many great authors have written about painting, and this is convincing evidence for the high regard in which it was held. But I would not have us carry this discussion any further. So let it be enough simply to state that it is fitting that our courtier should also have a knowledge of painting, since it is a worthy and beneficial art, and was greatly valued in the times when men were greater than now. And even if it had no other useful or pleasurable aspects, painting helps us to judge the merits of ancient and modern statues, of vases, buildings, medallions, cameos, intaglios and similar works, and it reveals the beauty of living bodies, with regard to both the delicacy of the countenance and the proportion of the other parts, in man as in all other creatures. So you see that a knowledge of painting is the source of very profound pleasure. And let those reflect on this who are so carried away when they see a beautiful woman that they think they are in paradise, and yet who cannot paint; for if they did know how to paint they would be all the more content, since they would then more perfectly discern the beauty that they find so agreeable.' . . .

The Choice of Companions

'It does not seem to me,' said signor Gaspare Pallavicino, 'that it is either right or indeed usual for people of quality to judge a man's character by this dress rather than by his words or actions, for in that case there would be many mistakes; and there is good reason for the proverb which says that the habit does not make the monk.'

'I am not saying,' replied Federico, 'that clothes provide the basis for making hard and fast judgements about a man's character, or that we cannot discover far more from someone's words and actions than from his attire. But I do maintain that a man's attire is also no small evidence for what kind of personality he has, allowing that it can sometimes prove misleading. Moreover, habits and manners, as well as actions and words, provide clues to the quality of the man.'

'And on what kind of things, other than words or actions, do you suggest we can base our judgement?' asked signor Gaspare.

Federico replied: 'I think you are splitting hairs. But to explain what I mean; there are some activities which still endure after they have been completed, such as building and writing, and there are others which do not endure, and those are what I am thinking of now. Thus in this sense I do not call walking, laughing, looking and so forth, activities, and yet all these external things often provide information about what is within. Tell me, didn't you decide that that friend of ours of whom we were speaking only this morning was a conceited and frivolous man, as soon as you saw him walking with that head-tossing and wriggling about, and smiling invitations to all and sundry to doff their caps to him? So too, whenever you see someone staring too intently, with blank eyes like an idiot, or laughing stupidly like those goitred mutes of the mountains of Bergamo, even though he doesn't say or do anything else, don't you take him for a great oaf? Do you not see, therefore, that these habits and manners, which for the moment I do not think of as acts, are in great part what men are known by?

'But there is another thing which seems to me greatly to damage or enhance a man's reputation, and this is his choice of really intimate friends. For to be sure it stands to reason that persons who are joined together in close amity and indissoluble companionship should also conform in their wishes, thoughts, opinions and aptitudes. So a man who associates with the ignorant or wicked is taken to be ignorant or wicked; and, on the other hand, a man who associates with those who are good, wise and discreet, is taken for such himself. For it seems natural for like to attract like. Hence I think it is right to take great care in forming these friendships, for of two close friends whoever knows one immediately assumes the other to be the same character.'

To this, Pietro Bembo answered: 'In contracting such intimate friendships as you describe it certainly seems to me that one ought to be extremely careful, not only because of the question of enhancing or damaging one's reputation but also because nowadays there are very few true friends to be found. Indeed, I doubt whether there exist in the world any more a Pylades and Orestes, a Theseus and Pirithous, or a Scipio and Laelius. Rather, I wonder by what fate it happens every day that two friends, after years of heartfelt and mutual affection, will end by deceiving one another in some way or other, either from malice or envy or inconstancy or some other evil motive. And they heap on each other the blame both doubtless deserve. Thus for my own part I have more than once been deceived by the person I loved most and of whose love, above everyone else's, I have been most confident; and because of this I have sometimes thought to myself that it may be as well never to trust anyone in this world nor to give oneself as a hostage to a friend, however dear and cherished he may be, to the extent of telling him all one's thoughts without reserve as if he were one's very self. For there are so many concealed places and recesses in our minds that it is humanly impossible to discover and judge the pretences hidden there. So I believe that it may be right to love and serve one person above all others, according to merit and worth, but never to trust so much in this tempting trap of friendship as to have cause to repent of it later on.'

BEHAVIOUR AMONG FRIENDS

Then Federico remarked: 'But certainly the loss would be far greater than the gain if from human intercourse should be removed that supreme degree of friendship which, I maintain, contains the best of life. Therefore I can in no way allow that what you say is reasonable; on the contrary, I would go so far as to maintain, for the most cogent reasons, that without this perfect friendship men would be the unhappiest of all creatures; and because some profane persons sully the sacred name of friendship, this does not mean that we should uproot it from our souls and because of the faults of the wicked deprive the good of so much happiness. And it is my opinion that here in our midst may be found more than one pair of friends, whose love is constant and without deceit, and bound to endure in all its intimacy until death, no less than if they were those of the ancient world whom you named earlier on. This is what happens when one chooses for a friend someone of similar ways, apart from the influence of the stars; and all that I have said I mean as regards good and virtuous persons, since the friendship of wicked men is not friendship at all. I also belive that the bond of friendship should not involve more than two people, for otherwise it could perhaps be dangerous. The reason for this is that, as you know, harmony is more difficult to achieve with several instruments than with two. I wish our courtier, therefore, to have a sincere and intimate friend of his own, if possible, of the kind we have described; and then that he should love, honour and respect all his other friends, according to their worth and merits, and also endeavour to associate more with those who are highly esteemed and noble and recognized as virtuous than with the ignoble and those of little worth, so that he in turn may be loved and honoured by them. And he will succeed in this if he is courteous, compassionate, generous, affable and charming as a companion, lively and diligent in serving and forwarding the advantage and honour of his friends, whether they are absent or present, tolerating their natural and excusable defects, without breaking with them for trifling reasons, and correcting in himself the defects that are amicably pointed out to him. He will succeed by never pushing in front of others to secure the first and most honoured place and by never doing as some do, who affect to despise the world and wish to lay down the law to everyone with a certain tiresome severity, and who, as well as being contentious over every little thing at all the wrong times, seek to censure what they do not do themselves and always find cause to complain of their friends, which is a detestable habit.'

After Federico had fallen silent, signor Gaspare Pallavicino began as follows:

'I should like you to go into rather more detail than you have done on the subject of behaviour between friends, for truly you talk very much in generalities and seem to discuss everything, as it were, merely in passing.'

'What do you mean, "in passing"?' replied Federico. 'Do you perhaps want me to tell you as well the very words you ought to use? Do you not agree that we have said enough on the subject?'

'Enough, I think,' answered signor Gaspare. 'But I should like to hear some more particulars concerning the manner in which men and women ought to converse among themselves. For in my opinion this is of considerable importance, seeing that at Court this is the chief occupation for most of the time, and if it never varied it would soon become tiresome.'

'It seems to me,' replied Federico, 'that we have given the courtier a knowledge of so many subjects that he can readily vary his conversation a great deal and adapt himself to the qualities of those with whom he has dealings, assuming that he possesses good judgement and allows himself to be ruled by that, and, depending on the circumstances, attends sometimes to grave matters and sometimes to festivities and games.'

'And which games?' asked signor Gaspare.

Federico answered with a laugh: 'For this, let us go for advice to Fra Serafino, who invents new ones every day.'

'Joking apart,' answered signor Gaspare, 'does it seem to you that it is wrong for the courtier to play at cards and dice?'

'To me, no,' said Federico, 'unless he does so too assiduously, and in consequence neglects things of greater importance, or indeed for no other reason than to win money and cheat his partner, and then, when he loses, is so dismayed and angry as to prove his avarice.'

Signor Gaspare replied: 'And what do you say about the game of chess?'

'That is certainly a refined and ingenious recreation,' said Federico, 'but it seems to me to possess one defect; namely, that is is possible for it to demand too much knowledge, so that anyone who wishes to become an outstanding player must, I think, give to it as much time and study as he would to learning some noble science or performing well something or other of importance; and yet for all his pains when all is said and done all he knows is a game. Therefore as far as chess is concerned we reach what is a very rare conclusion: that mediocrity is more to be praised than excellence.'

Signor Gaspare replied: 'But there are to be found many Spaniards who excel at chess and at a number of other games, and yet do not study them too exhaustively or neglect other things.'

'You may take it for granted,' said Federico, 'that they put in a great deal of study, but they conceal it. However, the other games you mention, apart from chess, are doubtless like many I have seen played which are of little moment and serve only to make the common people marvel; so I do not consider they deserve any praise or reward other than what Alexander the Great gave to the man who at some distance was so good at impaling chickpeas on a pin.

A GOOD REPUTATION

'But because it seems that Fortune, in this as in so many other things, has great influence on men's opinions, we sometimes see that a gentleman, however finely endowed and gifted he may be, proves disagreeable to his lord and always, as we say, raises his gall; and this is for no discernible reason. Thus when he comes into his lord's presence, and before he has been recognized by the others, though his conversation may be fluent and ready and though his behaviour, gestures and words and everything else may be all that can be desired, his lord will show that he has no high regard for him and, indeed, will display contempt. And as an immediate result of this, the others will at once fall in line with the wishes of the prince and to each one of them it will seem that the man is worthless; nor will there be found any to value or respect him, or laugh at his witticisms or regard him as being of any account; on the contrary, they will all immediately start to mock him and hound him down. Nor will it do the wretch any good to answer agreeably and well or take what is being said in good part, since they will all, down to the page-boys themselves, set about him so that even if he were the worthiest man in the world he would still be hounded down and frustrated. In contrast to this, if the prince should show that he favours some ignorant fellow, who knows neither how to speak or behave, often his manners and ways, however foolish and uncouth they may be, will be praised to the skies by everyone and the whole Court will seem to admire and respect him, and everyone will laugh at his jokes and at certain flat and boorish sayings calculated to make people feel sick rather than entertained. This is the extent to which men obstinately adhere to opinions engendered by the favour or disfavour of princes. Therefore I should wish our courtier to bolster up his inherent worth with skill and cunning, and ensure that whenever he has to go where he is a stranger and unknown he is preceded by a good reputation and that it becomes known that elsewhere, among other lords, ladies and knights, he is very highly regarded. For the fame which appears to rest on the opinions of many fosters a certain unshakeable belief in a man's worth which is then easily maintained and strengthened in minds already thus disposed and prepared. Moreover, by taking these steps the courtier avoids the annoyance I always feel when I am asked who I am and what my name is.' . . .

After pausing for a moment, the Magnifico then added
with a laugh:

'Do you not know that this proposition is held in philosophy: namely, that those who are weak in body are
able in mind? So there can be no doubt that being weaker
in body women are abler in mind and more capable of
speculative thought than men.'

Then he continued: 'But apart from this, since you have
said that I should argue from their acts as to the perfection of the one and the other, I say that if you will consider the operations of Nature, you will find that she
produces women the way they are not by chance but
adapted to the necessary end; for although she makes
them gentle in body and placid in spirit, and with many
other qualities opposite to those of men, yet the attributes
of the one and the other tend towards the same beneficial
end. For just as their gentle frailty makes women less
courageous, so it makes them more cautious; and thus the
mother nourishes her children, whereas the father in-
structs them and with his strength wins outside the home
what his wife, no less commendably, conserves with diligence and care. Therefore if you study ancient and modern history (although men have always been very sparing
in their praises of women) you will find that women as
well as men have constantly given proof of their worth;
and also that there had been some women who have
waged wars and won glorious victories, governed kingdoms with the greatest prudence and justice, and done all

that men have done. As for learning, cannot you recall reading of many women who knew philosophy, of others who have been consummate poets, others who prosecuted, accused and defended before judges with great eloquence? It would take too long to talk of the work they have done with their hands, nor is there any need for me to provide examples of it. So if in essential substance men are no more perfect than women, neither are they as regards accidents; and apart from theory this is quite clear in practice. And so I cannot see how you define this perfection of theirs.

'Now you said that Nature's intention is always to produce the most perfect things, and therefore she would if possible always produce men, and that women are the result of some mistake or defect rather than of intention. But I can only say that I deny this completely. You cannot possibly argue that Nature does not intend to produce the women without whom the human race cannot be preserved, which is something that Nature desires above everything else. For by means of the union of male and female, she produces children, who then return the benefits received in childhood by supporting their parents when they are old; then they renew them when they themselves have children, from whom they expect to receive in their old age what they bestowed on their own parents when they were young. In this way Nature, as if moving in a circle, fills out eternity and confers immortality on mortals. And since woman is as necessary to this process as man, I do not see how it can be that one is more the fruit of mere chance than the other. It is certainly true that

Nature always intends to produce the most perfect things, and therefore always intends to produce the species man, though not male rather than female; and indeed, if Nature always produced males this would be imperfection: for just as there results from body and soul a composite nobler than its parts, namely, man himself, so from the union of male and female there results a composite that preserves the human species, and without which its parts would perish. Thus male and female always go naturally together, and one cannot exist without the other. So by very definition we cannot call anything male unless it has its female counterpart, or anything female if it has no male counterpart. And since one sex alone shows imperfection, the ancient theologians attribute both sexes to God. For this reason, Orpheus said that Jove was both male and female; and we read in Holy Scripture that God made male and female in His own likeness; and very often when the poets speak of the gods they confuse the sex.'

MALE AND FEMALE

Then signor Gaspare said: 'I do not wish to go into such subtleties because these ladies would not understand them; and though I were to refute you with excellent arguments, they would still think that I was wrong, or pretend to at least; and they would at once give a verdict in their own favour. However, since we have made a beginning, I shall say only that, as you know, it is the opinion of very learned men that man is as the form and woman as the matter, and therefore just as form is more perfect than matter, and indeed it gives it its being, so man is far more perfect than woman. And I recall having once heard that a great philosopher in certain of his *Problems* asks: Why is it that a woman always naturally loves the man to whom she first gave herself in love? And on the contrary, why is it that a man detests the woman who first coupled with him in that way? And in giving his explanation he affirms that this is because in the sexual act the woman is perfected by the man, whereas the man is made imperfect, and that everyone naturally loves what makes him perfect and detests what makes him imperfect. Moreover, another convincing argument for the perfection of man and the imperfection of woman is that without exception every woman wants to be a man, by reason of a certain instinct that teaches her to desire her own perfection.'

The Magnifico Guiliano at once replied:

'The poor creatures do not wish to become men in order to make themselves more perfect but to gain their freedom and shake off the tyranny that men have imposed on them by their one-sided authority. Besides, the analogy you give of matter and form is not always applicable; for woman is not perfected by man in the way that matter is perfected by form. To be sure, matter receives its being from form, and cannot exist without it; and indeed the more material a form is, the more imperfect it is, and it is most perfect when separated from matter. On the other hand, woman does not receive her being from man but rather perfects him just as she is perfected by him, and thus both join together for the purpose of procreation which neither can ensure alone. Moreover, I shall attribute woman's enduring love for the man with whom she has first been, and man's detestation for the first woman he possesses, not to what is alleged by your philosopher in his *Problems* but to the resolution and constancy of women and the inconstancy of men. And for this, there are natural reasons: for because of its hot nature, the male sex possesses the qualities of lightness, movement and inconstancy, whereas from its coldness, the female sex derives its steadfast gravity and calm and is therefore more susceptible.'

At this point, signora Emilia turned to the Magnifico to say:

'In heaven's name, leave all this business of matter and form and male and female for once, and speak in a way that you can be understood. We heard and understood quite well all the evil said about us by signor Ottaviano and signor Gaspare, but now we can't at all understand your way of defending us. So it seems to me that what you are saying is beside the point and merely leaves in everyone's mind the bad impression of us given by these enemies of ours.'

'Do not call us that,' said signor Gaspare, 'for your real enemy is the Magnifico who, by praising women falsely, suggests they cannot be praised honestly.'

Then the Magnifico Guiliano continued: 'Do not doubt, madam, that an answer will be found for everything. But I don't want to abuse men as gratuitously as they have abused women; and if there were anyone here who happened to write these discussions down, I should not wish it to be thought later on, in some place where the concepts of matter and form might be understood, that the arguments and criticisms of signor Gaspare had not been refuted."

"I don't see," said signor Gaspare, "how on this point you can deny that man's natural qualities make him more perfect than woman, since women are cold in temperament and men are hot. For warmth is far nobler and more perfect than cold, since it is active and productive; and, as you know, the heavens shed warmth on the earth rather than coldness, which plays no part in the work of Nature. And so I believe that the coldness of women is the reason why they are cowardly and timid.'

'So you still want to pursue these sophistries,' replied the Magnifico Guiliano, 'though I warn you that you get the worst of it every time. Just listen to this, and you'll understand why. I concede that in itself warmth is more perfect than cold; but this is not therefore the case with things that are mixed and composite, since if it were so the warmer any particular substance was the more perfect it would be, whereas in fact temperate bodies are the most perfect. Let me inform you also that women are cold in temperament only in comparison with men. In themselves, because of their excessive warmth, men are far from temperate; but in themselves women are temperate, or at least more nearly temperate than men, since they possess, in proportion to their natural warmth, a degree of moisture which in men, because of their excessive aridity, soon evaporates without trace. The coldness which women possess also counters and moderates their natural warmth, and brings it far nearer to a temperate condition; whereas in men excessive warmth soon brings their natural heat to the highest point where for lack of sustenance it dies away. And thus since men dry out more than women in the act of procreation they generally do not live so long; and therefore we can attribute another perfection to women, namely, that enjoying longer life than men they fulfil far better than men the intention of Nature. As for the warmth that is shed on us from the heavens, I have nothing to say, since it has only its name in common with what we are talking about and preserving as it does all things beneath the orb of the moon, both warm and cold, it cannot be opposed to coldness. But the timidity of women, though it betrays a degree of imperfection, has a noble origin in the subtlety and readiness of their senses which convey images very speedily to the mind, because of which they are easily moved by external things. Very often you will find men who have no fear of death or of anything else and yet cannot be called courageous, since they fail to recognize danger and rush headlong without another thought along the path they have chosen. This is the result of a certain obtuse insensitivity; and a fool cannot be called brave. Indeed, true greatness of soul springs from a deliberate choice and free resolve to act in a certain way and to set honour and duty above every possible risk, and from being so stout-hearted even in the face of death, that one's faculties do not fail or falter but perform their functions in speech and thought as if they were completely untroubled. We have seen and heard of great men of this sort, and also of many women, both in recent centuries and in the ancient world, who no less than men have shown greatness of spirit and have performed deeds worthy of infinite praise.' ...

PROVOCATIVE WOMEN

Having spoken in this way, the Magnifico then fell silent. And signor Gaspare remarked with a smile:

'Now you cannot complain that the signor Magnifico has not formed a truly excellent Court lady; and from now on, if any such lady be discovered, I declare that she deserves to be regarded as the equal of the courtier.'

Signor Emilia retorted: 'I will guarantee to discover her, if you will find the courtier.'

Roberto added: 'Certainly, no one can deny that the lady fashioned by signor Magnifico is most perfect. Nevertheless, with regard to those last qualities pertaining to love, I still think he has made her a little too hard, especially in wanting her, in her words, gestures and behaviour, to robe her lover of all hope and do all she can to plunge him into despair. For as everyone knows no men desire what is hopeless. Admittedly, there have been some women, proud perhaps of their worth and beauty, who have immediately told their suitors that they need not imagine they would ever get from them what they wanted. And yet subsequently they have been a little more gracious in their reception and the way they look, and thus their kindly behaviour has tended to modify their haughty words. But if this lady drives away all hope by her acts

37

and looks and behaviour, then I think that if he is wise our courtier will never love her, and so she will lack the perfection of having someone who does.'

To this, the Magnifico answered: 'I do not want this lady of mine to drive away hope altogether, but only when it comes to things that are dishonourable; and if the courtier is as courteous and modest as these gentlemen have made him, then he will not even desire such things, let alone hope for them. For if the courtier's love for her is prompted by the beauty, good way of life, talent, virtue, discernment and other commendable qualities with which we have endowed her, then his intention is bound to be virtuous too. Again, if the means by which the courtier is to win her favour are to be nobility, distinction in arms, letters and music, and gentleness and grace in speech and conversation, then the object of his love is bound to be of the same quality as the means through which it is attained. And then just as there exist various kinds of beauty so there exist various desires in men; and so many of them, when they chance to see a woman as grave and beautiful as the one we have described, whether she is passing by, or jesting or joking, or doing what you will, are completely abashed and hardly dare try to serve her because of the respect aroused in all who look at her by the grace which informs her every act. Their hopes aroused, they prefer to turn to those charming and provocative women, who are so frail and tender and whose words, acts and looks express a certain languid emotion that seems likely to turn easily into love. Others, to avoid disappointment, prefer to love the kind of woman who is so free in her eyes, words and movements as to do the first thing that comes to mind, acting with a certain revealing *naïveté*. And then there are those who believe that true achievement lies in overcoming difficulties and that the sweetest triumph is to capture what others think is impregnable; and these bold spirits readily fall in love with the beauties of those women whose eyes, words and ways suggest unusual severity, so as to prove that they are capable of overcoming all obstacles and forcing even rebellious and wilful women to love them. Men who are as self-confident as this, and therefore certain that they cannot be deceived, are also ready to love certain women whose beauty seems cunningly contrived to conceal all the wiles imaginable, or others whose beauty is accompanied by a scornful manner of few words and few smiles and an air of disdain for anyone who looks at them or serves them. And then there are other men who consent to love only those women whose countenance, speech and every movement bring together graciousness, courtesy, discernment and virtue, as if to form a single and exquisite flower. So if my Court lady fails to win the love of those whose intentions are impure, this does not mean that she will lack for lovers; for she will find many who are inspired both by her merits and their own worthiness, which will assure them that they deserve her affection.'

Roberto was continuing to argue, but the Duchess ruled that he was in the wrong and gave her approval to what the Magnifico had said; and then she added:

'We have no reason to complain of the Magnifico, since it is quite clear that the lady he has fashioned for us can bear comparison with the courtier and even has the advantage of him. For he has taught her how to love, and this is something these gentlemen have failed to do for their courtier.'

At this, the Unico Aretino remarked: 'It is certainly right to teach ladies how to love, because I've rarely encountered one who does know how to do so. And their beauty is nearly always accompanied by cruelty and ingratitude towards those who serve them most faithfully and whose nobility, gentleness and virtue deserve to be rewarded. Very often, too, they abandon themselves to the most stupid and worthless rascals, who despise rather than love them. So to help them avoid these gross errors perhaps it would have been as well to teach them first how to choose a man worthy of their love and only then how to love him. But this isn't necessary in the case of men, who know the answer only too well for themselves. I can vouch for this myself, for I was never taught to love but by the divine beauty and inspired manners of a lady whom I had no choice but to adore, and I had no need at all of any instruction or teacher. I believe this holds good for all those who are truly in love; and so it would be more suitable to teach the courtier how to make himself loved than how to love.'

'Well, do tell us about this,' said signora Emilia.

'It seems to me,' continued the Unico, 'to be only reasonable that men should win favour from their ladies by serving them and pleasing them; but what they consider serving and pleasing to consist in must, I think, be taught by the ladies themselves, since they often want such strange things that no man can think what they are, and indeed they often don't know themselves. So it would be very fitting, madam, if since you are a woman and ought to know what pleases women, you undertake the task yourself and put everyone in your debt.'

'But you enjoy such universal favour with women,' replied signora Emilia, 'that you must surely know all the ways in which their favour can be won. So it's fitting that you should teach them to others.'

'Madam,' replied the Unico, 'I could give a lover no more useful advice than that he should ensure that you have no influence on the lady whose favour he seeks; for such good qualities as everyone once thought were mine, together with the sincerest love that ever existed, have not had as much power to make me loved as you have had to make me hated.'

'Signor Unico,' replied Emilia, 'God keep me from thinking, much less doing, anything to make you hated. For not only would this be wrong, but I would be thought very silly if I attempted the impossible in that way. But since you urge me to say something about what is pleasing to women I shall do so; and if what I say displeases you, then you have only yourself to blame. I consider, then, that if a man is to be loved he must himself love and be lovable; and these two things are enough for him to win the favour of women. And to answer your accusation, I declare that everyone knows and sees that you are most lovable; but I am very doubtful as to whether you love as sincerely as you claim, and perhaps the others are too. For by being too lovable you have made yourself loved by many women. But when great rivers divide into several channels they dwindle to small streams; and in the same way when love is given to more than one object it loses much of its force. However, your own constant lamenting and accusations of ingratitude against the women you have served, which do not ring true, considering your great merits, are really designed as a kind of concealment to hide the favours, the joys and the pleasures you have known in love, and to reassure those women who love you and have abandoned themselves to you that you won't give them away. So they too are content that you should openly make a pretence of loving other women in order to conceal your genuine love for them. And so if the women you pretend to love now are not as credulous as you would wish, this is because your technique is beginning to be understood, and not because I cause you to be hated.'

Then the Unico remarked: 'I've no wish to go on disproving what you say, since as far as I can see I am as fated to be disbelieved when I speak the truth as you are to be believed when you tell lies.'

'But admit,' replied signora Emilia, 'that you do not love in the way you say. For if you did, you would desire only to please your lover and to wish only what she wishes, since this is the law of love. But the way you complain of her so much suggests deceit, as I said before, or indeed proves that your wishes are not the same as hers.'

'On the contrary,' said the Unico, 'I certainly wish whatever she wishes, and this proves that I love her; but I complain because she doesn't wish what I wish, and this, according to the rule you quoted, suggests that she doesn't love me.'

Then signora Emilia replied: 'But a man who begins to love must also begin to please the woman he loves and to be ruled by her in accommodating his every wish to hers. And he must ensure that his desires are all subordinate to hers and that his soul is the slave of hers, or indeed, if possible, that it is transformed into hers; and he should see this as being the greatest happiness he could want. For this is the way of those who are truly in love.'

'The greatest happiness for me,' said the Unico, 'would be precisely if a single will governed both her soul and mine.'

'Then you must bring this about,' replied signora Emilia.

DECLARATION OF LOVE

At this point, Bernardo interrupted to say:

'Certainly a man who is truly in love without any prompting by others devotes all his thoughts to serving and pleasing the woman he loves. But sometimes his devotion goes unrecognized, and so I think that as well as loving and serving he must demonstrate his love so clearly in some other way that the woman he loves cannot conceal that she knows she is loved; though he should do this so modestly as to avoid any suggestion of disrespect. And so, madam, since you were saying that a lover's soul should be the slave of the woman he loves, I implore you to teach us this secret too, as it seems to me extremely important.'

At this, Cesare smiled and remarked: 'If the lover is so modest that he is ashamed to declare his love, let him write it in a letter.'

'On the contrary,' said signora Emilia, 'if he is discreet as he ought to be, before he makes any declaration he should make sure that he won't offend her.'

Then signor Gaspare said: 'Well, all women like to be begged for their love, even though they mean to refuse what is asked of them.'

At this, the Magnifico Guiliano remarked: 'You are very much mistaken, and I would advise the courtier never to adopt this strategy, unless he is certain that he won't be repulsed.'

'Then what course should he follow?' asked signor Gaspare.

'Well, if he wants to speak or write,' continued the Magnifico, 'he should do so with such modesty and care that to start with his words seem wholly tentative and even ambiguous and affect her in such a way that she may legitimately pretend, if she wishes to avoid embarrassment, not to understand what is meant. Thus if he finds difficulties in the way, he can withdraw easily and pretend to have spoken or written with some other purpose in view, in order to enjoy safely those endearments and kindnesses that women often grant to those who seem to accept them as a mark of friendship but retract as soon as they perceive that they are interpreted as a demonstration of love. Hence those men who are too hasty and make their advances too presumptuously, with a kind of stubborn impetuosity, often lose these favours, and with good reason. For a true lady always considers she is being insulted when someone shows a lack of respect by seeking to gain her love before he has served her.

'Therefore in my view when the courtier wishes to declare his love he should do so by his actions rather than by speech, for a man's feelings are sometimes more clearly revealed by a sigh, a gesture of respect or a certain shyness than by volumes of words. And next he should use his eyes to carry faithfully the message written in his heart, because they often communicate hidden feelings more effectively than anything else, including the tongue and the written word. In doing this, they not only reveal the lover's thoughts but often arouse affection in the heart of the one he loves. For the vital spirits that dart from his eyes originate near the heart, and thus when they penetrate the eyes of the woman he loves like an arrow speeding to its target they go straight to her heart, as if to their true abode; and there they mingle with those other vital spirits and with the very subtle kind of blood which these contain, and in this way they infect the blood near to the heart to which they have come, warming it and making it like themselves and ready to receive the impression of the image they carry with them. In this way, journeying back and forth from the eyes to the heart, and bringing back the tinder and steel of beauty and grace, with the breath of desire these messengers kindle the fire which never dies, since it is fed on constant hope. So one can truly say that eyes are the guides of love, especially if they are graceful and soft, and blue in colour or a limpid and shining black, full of gaiety and laughter and in their gaze gracious and penetrating, like some so profound that one seems to see down to the heart itself. Thus we find that a woman's eyes wait like soldiers in ambush while her body, if it is beautiful and well proportioned, attracts and draws close to itself anyone who sees it from afar; and then as soon as he is near by the eyes dart forth and bewitch him like sorcerers, especially when they send their rays into the eyes of the beloved person just as his are doing the same; for then the vital spirits meet each other and in that sweet encounter each takes on the qualities of the other, as we find in the case of a diseased eye which, by staring hard at a healthy eye, gives it the disease from which it is suffering. So it seems to me that this is the way in which our courtier can, in great part, make his love known. It is true that unless they are carefully governed, the eyes frequently reveal amorous desires to someone whom one would wish to keep in ignorance, because they make deep passion almost visible and thus betray it to others than the one whom it concerns. So a man who has not lost the bridle of reason will govern himself cautiously, paying attention to time and place, and, when necessary, he will abstain from gazing too intently, however hungrily he desires to do so: for there is no joy in love that is known to all.' . . .

Then Cesare Gonzaga remarked: 'Well, I don't know what virtues appropriate for a ruler can spring from temperance, if temperance, as you say, removes all the emotions from one's mind. This might be fitting in a hermit or a monk; but I can hardly think that it is becoming for a prince, who is magnanimous, liberal and valiant in arms, whatever the provocation, never to display anger or hatred or indeed kindliness or scorn or lust or any emotion at all. For how could he otherwise exert any authority either over his people or his troops?'

Signor Ottaviano replied: 'I did not say that temperance completely removes and uproots the emotions from a man's soul, nor would it be well for it to do so, since there are good elements even in the emotions. But what it does do is to make what is perverse and opposed to right conduct in the emotions responsive to reason. So it is not right, in order to remove conflicts, to extirpate the emotions altogether; for this would be like trying to suppress drunkenness by legislating against the use of wine, or forbidding anyone to run since when they do men sometimes fall over. You are well aware that when someone is breaking in a horse he does not stop it from running or jumping but ensures that it does so at the right time and at the command of the rider. So when they are moderated by temperance the emotions are conducive to virtue, just as wrath strengthens fortitude, hatred against wicked men strengthens justice, and the other emotions strengthen other kinds of virtue. And if they were killed altogether,

47

this would leave the reason weak and languid, so that it would be ineffectual, like the captain of a ship that is becalmed after the winds have dropped. So do not be so surprised, Cesare, if I said that temperance is the cause of many other virtues; for when a man's soul is attuned to this harmony, reason makes it readily receptive to true fortitude which in turn makes it intrepid and unassailable, and immune to human suffering. And this is just as true of justice, the pure friend of modesty and goodness, and the queen of all the virtues, because justice teaches us to do what should be done and to eschew what is wrong. Thus justice is wholly perfect, since the other virtues perform their work through her, and she benefits both the just man and others as well. And without justice, as it is said, Jove himself could not govern his kingdom well. These virtues are also followed by magnanimity, which enhances them all, though it cannot exist alone since anyone lacking other virtues cannot be magnanimous. And then for their guide, the virtues have prudence, which consists in a certain quality of judgement in making the right decisions. The other links in this happy chain of virtues are liberality, munificence, the desire of honor, gentleness, charm, affability and many other qualities there is not the time to name. But if our courtier behaves as we have suggested he will discover these flourishing in the soul of his prince, and every day will see blossoming there more delightful flowers and fruits than there are in all the lovely gardens on earth. He himself will know great contentment, when he reminds himself that he gave his prince not what fools give, namely, gifts such as gold and silver, vases and garments (of which the prince has too many already and the giver only too few) but what is doubtless the greatest and rarest of all human virtues: the manner and method of good government. This alone would be enough to make men happy and restore to earth the golden age which is said to have existed once, when Saturn ruled.'

MONARCHY OR REPUBLIC

After signor Ottaviano had paused for a moment as if to rest, signor Gaspare said:

'What you do think, signor Ottaviano, is the happier form of government and the more likely to restore the golden age that you mentioned: the single rule of a good prince, or the government of a good republic?'

Signor Ottaviano replied: 'I should always prefer the rule of a good prince, since this kind of dominion is more in accord with Nature and (if it is permissible to compare such small things with the infinite) more similar to that of God, who governs the universe by Himself alone. But leaving this aside, you notice that in all human creations, such as armies, armadas, buildings and so forth, the whole is referred to one man who governs as he wishes; similarly, in our bodies all the members perform and carry out their functions according to the decisions taken by the mind. Moreover, it seems fitting that people should be ruled in this way by one head, as are many of the animals, to whom Nature teaches this obedience as a most salutary thing. Notice how deer, like cranes and many other birds, when they migrate always choose a single leader to follow and obey; and the bees, almost as if they could reason, obey their royal leader as respectfully as the most law-abiding people on earth. And all this goes to prove conclusively that government by a prince is more in accord with Nature than that of a republic.'

At this, Pietro Bembo remarked: 'But it seems to me that, since God has given us the supreme gift of freedom, it is wrong that it should be taken from us or that one man's share should be greater than another's. Yet this is what happens when there is government by princes, who, for the most part keep their subjects under the strictest surveillance, whereas in well-constituted republics this freedom is always conserved. Moreover, in judgements and deliberations, it more often happens that the opinion of a single man is false than that of many; for, because of anger or indignation or lust, a single man is more prone to lose his equanimity than a multitude, which is like a vast expanse of water and therefore less subject to contamination than a small quantity. I must add that I am not convinced that the examples you give from the animal world are applicable: for the deer and the cranes and all the others do not always prefer to follow and obey a single leader. On the contrary, they change and vary their behaviour, giving full authority now to one from among them and now to another; and in this way they are organized more in the style of a republic than of a monarchy. Indeed this can be called freedom among true equals, when those who sometimes command, sometimes obey as well. Likewise, the example of the bees does not seem relevant to me, for their royal leader is not of the same species; and therefore whoever wished to give men a truly worthy lord would have to choose him from another species, endowed with a nature superior to ours, if they are reasonably bound to obey him, like the herd which obeys not an animal of its own but a herdsman who is human and therefore of a superior species. Because of what I have said, signor Ottaviano, I think that a republic is a more desirable form of government than a monarchy.'

'In contradiction,' answered signor Ottaviano, 'I will deploy just one argument, namely, that there are only three forms of sound government: monarchy, the rule of the good (in the ancient world called the *optimates*) and government by the citizens. And the degenerate and lawless forms taken by these systems when they are ruined and corrupted are, in place of monarchy, tyranny, in place of the best, government by a few powerful men, and in place of the citizens, government by the common people, which wrecks the constitution and surrenders complete power to the control of the multitude. Of these three bad forms of government, there is no doubt that tyranny is the worst, as could be proved by many arguments; and so it follows that of the three good forms of government, monarchy is best, being the opposite of the worst. (For as you know, contrary causes produce contrary effects.) Now, in regard to what you said concerning freedom, I reply that it should not be said that true freedom consists in living as one wishes but rather in living under good laws. Nor is it any less natural and useful and necessary to obey than to command; and some things are born and devised and ordained by Nature to obey, just as others are to command. It is true that there are two ways of exercising rule: one is arbitrary and violent, like that of masters over their slaves, or the way the soul commands the body; the other way is milder and gentler, like that of good princes ruling their citizens through the laws, or the way reason commands our desires. Both of these ways are useful, for the body is naturally so constituted as to obey the soul, and likewise man's desires to obey his reason. There are also many men concerned solely with physical activities, and these differ from men versed in the things of the mind as much as the soul differs from the body. As rational creatures, however, they share in reason to the extent of being able to recognize it; but they do not possess it themselves or profit from it. These, then, are essentially slaves, and it is more advantageous for them to obey than to command.' ...

BODY AND SOUL

Then signor Gaspare said: 'Signor Ottaviano, you have gone out of your way to praise good education and have indicated that you think it is the principal means for attaining virtue and goodness. So I would like to know whether the instruction which the courtier must give his prince should be conveyed casually during the ordinary conduct of affairs, so as to accustom him to acting in the right way without his being aware of it, or should be conveyed at the outset by formal argument about the nature of good and evil, and explanations, before the prince proceeds any farther, as to what is the right path to follow and what he must avoid. In short, should the prince be encouraged and confirmed in a virtuous way of life through argument and theory, or through practice?'

'You are involving me in too long a discussion,' answered signor Ottaviano. 'However, so that you don't think I want to avoid answering your questions, let me say that just as we are divided into soul and body, so the soul is divided into two parts, one of which contains our reason and the other our instinct. And then just as in generation the body precedes the soul, so the irrational part of the soul precedes the rational; and this we see clearly in the case of children in whom anger and desire are evident almost as soon as they are born, whereas reason appears only with the passing of time. So we must take care for the body before the soul, and for the instincts before the reason, though this is in the first case for the sake of the soul and in the second for the sake of the reason. For just as intellectual virtue is perfected by teaching, so moral virtue is perfected by practice. First, therefore, the prince should learn through practice, which will make it possible for him to govern the instincts that are not yet susceptible to reason and through this commendable discipline direct them towards a worthy end. Then they should be moulded by the intellect, which sheds light at a later stage but enables all the virtues to be perfected in one whose soul has been strengthened through good habits which, in my opinion, are fundamental.'

Then signor Gaspare commented: 'Before you go any

further, I would like to know what attention should be paid to the body, because you did say that we should care for the body before the soul.'

Signor Ottaviano replied with a smile: 'Ask those you see here who nourish their bodies so well and look so fat and well; for mine, as you see, is not too well cared for. However, one could also talk about this at some length, as about the proper time for marrying, so that the children are neither too near nor too far from their fathers' age, and about the games and education necessary from the time of birth onwards so that they grow up handsome, healthy and strong.'

Signor Gaspare answered: 'In my opinion, what women would most like so that their children should grow up handsome and attractive would be to have them in common in the fashion that Plato urges in his *Republic*.'

Then Signora Emilia said with a laugh: 'It's against the rules for you to begin criticizing women again.'

'But I mean to praise them highly,' replied signor Gaspare, 'by saying that they are in favour of a custom approved by such a great man.'

Cesare added with a laugh: 'Let us see whether this custom may be included among signor Ottaviano's teachings (for I do not know whether he has yet stated all of them) and if the prince should make it a law.'

'Well,' answered signor Ottaviano, 'the few I have stated would doubtless be enough to make the prince as good as those we find nowadays can be, though if one wished to go into details there would be far more to say.'

Then the Duchess added: 'Since words cost nothing, do

please tell us all that comes to your mind in the matter of instructing your prince.'

Signor Ottaviano replied: 'Madam, I would teach him many other things, if only I knew them. And one of them would be that from among his subjects he should choose several of the noblest and wisest gentlemen, whom he should always consult, and that he should give them free leave and authority to tell him their opinion on any subject without hesitation; and he should so behave towards them that everyone would realize he wanted to know the truth about everything and detested lies. Apart from this council of nobles, I would advise him to choose from among the people others of lower rank to constitute a popular council and confer with the nobles concerning the affairs of the city, whether public or private. And in this way the prince, as the head, and the nobles and people, as the members, would form a single united body, the government of which would depend chiefly on the prince, yet would also include the others. And then this state would have the constitution of all three good forms of government, namely, monarchy, rule by the best and rule by the people.

RELIGION

'Next, I should show him that of all the responsibilities that fall to a prince, the most important is justice. And to maintain this, there should be appointed to hold office men of wisdom and probity, who must be good as well as judicious, for otherwise their sagacity is merely cunning; indeed, when goodness is lacking, the skill and subtlety of the prosecutors means simply the ruin and destruction of law and justice, and then the blame for all their errors must fall on the one who has placed them in office. I should inform the prince that it is justice which inspires the reverence for God which is due to Him from all, and especially from rulers who should love Him above all else and direct all their actions to Him as being their true end. And, as Xenophon said, they should always honour and love Him, though especially when they are prospering so that they may all the more confidently pray for His mercy in times of adversity. For it is impossible to govern either oneself or others well without the help of God, who to the good sometimes sends good fortune as His minister, to protect them against grave dangers, and sometimes adverse fortune to prevent their being so lulled by prosperity that they forget Him or human prudence, which often offsets ill fortune as a good player remedies bad throws of the dice by the way he places the board. Nor would I fail to remind the prince that he should be truly religious, but not superstitious or given to the folly of spells and fortune-telling; for if he combines true religion and reverence for God with human prudence he will also enjoy good fortune and the protection of God, always disposed to increase his prosperity in times of peace or war.

'Next, I should tell him that he should love his country and his people, and not rule too oppressively, lest this should make him hateful to them; for this encourages sedition, conspiracy and a thousand other evils. Nor yet too tolerantly, lest he should become despised; and this encourages a dissolute and licentious life on the part of his subjects, rapine, theft, murder and disrespect for the laws, and often the total destruction and ruin of cities and kingdoms. Next, that he should love those near to him, according to their rank, observing in some things, such as justice and liberty, a strict equality; and in other things a reasonable inequality, as in being generous, in rewarding, in distributing honours and dignities, according to the differences in their merits, which should always be less rather than greater than the rewards they receive. In this way he would be not merely loved but almost adored by his subjects; nor to protect his life would he need to trust himself to foreigners, since for their own sake his own people would guard it with their own, and everyone would readily obey the laws, seeing that the prince obeyed them himself and was, as it were, their custodian and incorruptible executor. In this respect, he should command such confidence that, even if sometimes it were necessary to go against them in some manner, everyone would understand that he did it to good purpose, and his wishes would command the same respect and reverence as the laws themselves. In consequence, the minds of the citizens would be so tempered that the good would not seek to have more than they needed, and the bad could not do so. For very often excessive riches are the cause of great calamities; as in poor Italy, which has been and still is the helpless prey of foreign troops, on account both of bad government and of its abundant wealth. So it would be advisable for most of the citizens to be neither very rich nor very poor, since those who are too rich often become proud and reckless, and the poor cowardly and dishonest. But those of moderate wealth neither seek to ensnare others nor risk being ensnared themselves; being the majority, they are also more powerful; and therefore neither the poor nor the rich can conspire against the prince or stir up sedition. So to avoid this evil, it is very salutary to keep everyone in a middle way of life.

'I would maintain, therefore, that the prince should adopt these and various other appropriate policies so that his subjects should not begin to hanker after new things or a change in government, which they invariably do either in the hope of some gain or indeed honour, or from fear of loss or shame. This restlessness is inspired sometimes by a desperate hatred and anger aroused by the injuries and insults they suffer because of the greed, insolence and cruelty, or the lust, of those who are over them; sometimes by the contempt that is fostered by the neglect, cowardice and worthlessness of princes. These two errors should be avoided by winning the love and allegiance of the people; and this is done by favouring and rewarding the good and by prudently, and sometimes severely, preventing the evil and seditious from growing powerful, something which is easier to do beforehand than it is to crush them once they are strong. I should say that to prevent the people falling into such errors the best way is not to allow them to adopt evil practices, and especially those which become established gradually; for these are the hidden plagues which destroy cities before they can be remedied or even detected. I should advise the prince to endeavour by these policies to keep his subjects tranquil and to ensure that they enjoy spiritual and physical well-being and constant prosperity, the last, however, being promoted for the sake of the former, since unlike bodily well-being and good fortune, spiritual riches are more advantageous the greater and more copious they are. Then if his subjects are good and worthy, and properly directed towards the goal of happiness, the prince will be a very great lord; for it is a great and true dominion in which the subjects are good, properly governed and well ordered.'

TRUE GREATNESS

At this, signor Gaspare remarked: 'If all the prince's subjects were good, then I think he would be only a petty lord, seeing that the good never number more than a few.'

Signor Ottaviano answered: 'If some Circe were to turn all the subjects of the King of France into wild beasts, would you not consider that he would then be only a petty lord, even ruling over so many thousands of creatures? And on the other hand, if all the flocks pastured on these mountains of ours were to turn into wise men and valorous knights, wouldn't you consider that the herdsmen in charge of them, and by whom they were obeyed, had become great lords? So you see that it is not the number of their subjects but their worth that makes princes great.'

READ MORE IN PENGUIN

For complete information about books available from Penguin and how to order them, please write to us at the appropriate address below. Please note that for copyright reasons the selection of books varies from country to country.

IN THE UNITED KINGDOM: Please write to *Dept. EP, Penguin Books Ltd, Bath Road, Harmondsworth, Middlesex UB7 0DA.*

IN THE UNITED STATES: Please write to *Consumer Sales, Penguin USA, P.O. Box 999, Dept. 17109, Bergenfield, New Jersey 07621-0120.* VISA and MasterCard holders call 1-800-253-6476 to order Penguin titles.

IN CANADA: Please write to *Penguin Books Canada Ltd, 10 Alcorn Avenue, Suite 300, Toronto, Ontario M4V 3B2.*

IN AUSTRALIA: Please write to *Penguin Books Australia Ltd, P.O. Box 257, Ringwood, Victoria 3134.*

IN NEW ZEALAND: Please write to *Penguin Books (NZ) Ltd, Private Bag 102902, North Shore Mail Centre, Auckland 10.*

IN INDIA: Please write to *Penguin Books India Pvt Ltd, 706 Eros Apartments, 56 Nehru Place, New Delhi 110 019.*

IN THE NETHERLANDS: Please write to *Penguin Books Netherlands bv, Postbus 3507, NL-1001 AH Amsterdam.*

IN GERMANY: Please write to *Penguin Books Deutschland GmbH, Metzlerstrasse 26, 60594 Frankfurt am Main.*

IN SPAIN: Please write to *Penguin Books S. A., Bravo Murillo 19, 1° B, 28015 Madrid.*

IN ITALY: Please write to *Penguin Italia s.r.l., Via Felice Casati 20, I-20124 Milano.*

IN FRANCE: Please write to *Penguin France S. A., 17 rue Lejeune, F-31000 Toulouse.*

IN JAPAN: Please write to *Penguin Books Japan, Ishikiribashi Building, 2-5-4, Suido, Bunkyo-ku, Tokyo 112.*

IN GREECE: Please write to *Penguin Hellas Ltd, Dimocritou 3, GR-106 71 Athens.*

IN SOUTH AFRICA: Please write to *Longman Penguin Southern Africa (Pty) Ltd, Private Bag X08, Bertsham 2013.*